CHARLES V

Katherine Brice

Published by Horsham House
ISBN 978-0-908346-07-3

AUCKLAND - WELLINGTON
www.horshamhouse.com

First published in 1988
Reprint 2015

© Copyright 2015 Katherine Brice.
ISBN 978-0-908346-07-3

Published by Horsham House of New Zealand, a division of Horsham House Limited. PO Box 92, Waimauku, Auckland 0842. **www.horshamhouse.com**.

Cover illustration designed by Horsham House Limited.

Charles V

1. Introduction

'Roman King, future Emperor, semper augustus, King of Spain, Sicily, Jerusalem, the Balearic Islands, the Canary Islands, the Indies and the mainland on the far shore of the Atlantic, Archduke of Austria, Duke of Burgundy, Brabant, Styria, Carinthia, Carniola, Luxembourg. Limburg, Athens, and Patras, Count of Habsburg, Flanders and Tyrol, Count Palatine of Burgundy, Hainault, Pfirt, Roussillon, Landgrave of Alsace, Count of Swabia, Lord of Asia and Africa.'

Thus ran the titles of Charles I of Spain, more commonly known as Charles V, the Holy Roman Emperor. The list conveys the extent of territories stretching from Spain to Italy, Austria, the Netherlands and Franche-Comté and, across the ocean, the vast, only partly discovered bulk of the New World. Some of the titles are purely honorific, such as Lord of Africa and Asia, while the title 'Roman King, future Emperor' conveyed great prestige but no territory. The latter is very important. By virtue of his titles Charles could legitimately see himself as the leader of Christendom with all that would entail in the fight against the Infidel and heresy; but the support for such a claim to leadership came from a strictly limited territorial base, albeit one that dwarfed the possessions of any other European ruler.

The key to Charles V's empire lay not in conquest but in dynasty. It was an accident of inheritance that indicates the second vital point about Charles V's empire, which is also revealed in the list of his titles. The only link between the territories was the person of Charles himself. In each dominion he had a different position (for, instance, King of Spain, Archduke of Austria, Count of Swabia) and there was no unity between them, hence the more accurate and contemporary term to describe his empire - 'monarchia'. Charles respected the individual traditions and privileges of his territories. This was unavoidable given the impossibility of fighting sustained opposition had he done otherwise, but it meant that no imperial institutions or financial systems were created which would have made his empire more manageable.

Charles was the eldest son of Philip of Burgundy and Joanna of Spain, sometime called Joanna the Mad. He spent his entire childhood in the Netherlands and became Duke of Burgundy at the age of six. The Burgundian court had an elaborate code of chivalry expressed in the order of the Golden Fleece and this heavily influenced Charles. He believed strongly in the idea of knightly honour and fighting for the Christian faith and this sometimes led him into naive behaviour, as in 1528 when he challenged Francis I to single combat for breaking his word over the Treaty of Madrid.

Charles believed he had received his inheritance from God as a sacred trust and it was his responsibility to maintain the unity of Christendom and to fight the Infidel. This view was shared by Mercurino Gattinara, his Imperial Chancellor from 1518 to 1530, who wrote to Charles immediately after his election as Emperor in 1519:

Sire, God has been very merciful to you: he has raised you above all the Kings and princes of Christendom to a power such as no sovereign has enjoyed since your ancestor Charles the Great (i.e. Charlemagne). He has set you on the way towards a world monarchy, towards the uniting of all Christendom under a single shepherd.

Unfortunately for Charles, the rest of Europe did not want a single shepherd, certainly not one who had the power to make the idea a reality. The emerging nations of England and France and the princes of Germany saw Charles' claims to overlordship as potentially threatening while the Pope, whose duty it was, according to Charles, to support him, could tolerate neither Charles' claim to be the arbiter of Europe's religious problems nor his pretensions to power in Italy. 'Successive popes were not sorry to see Charles V ruined by the problem of heresy whose resolution might have greatly increased his power' (N M Sutherland).

Thus the uniting of Christendom eluded Charles precisely because of the extent of his world monarchy. His power held out the prospect of success and yet at the same time snatched it away. However genuine his religious ideals, his potential allies in the struggle against the Protestants, the Pope and Catholic princes were reluctant to give him the necessary support to ensure success because of his political role.

It has been suggested that Charles was the victim of his inheritance, condemned to seek a prize that would always elude him because of the forces ranged against him. This is too simple a view; religion was not the only motive behind Charles' actions. The war against France always took precedence over defence of the Danube against the Turks and over the struggle against the German Protestants. It is important to consider whether this was putting his dynasty and inheritance first or whether Charles could legitimately justify his actions by putting the security of his frontiers above all other considerations.

Charles V had great power but this brought awesome responsibilities and the suspicion and potential hostility of the other powers of Europe. In general, Charles failed when the forces ranged against him were too great. But much depends on how Charles is viewed. The great biography by Karl Brandi which is the foundation of modern studies of Charles V focuses attention on Charles in northern Europe, where his setbacks were greatest. He might be thought more of a success if he is viewed as a Mediterranean monarch rather than as a world emperor.

2. Charles in Spain

In January 1516, Ferdinand of Aragon died and Charles became King with his mother Joanna the Mad, who lived on as a shadowy figure at Tordesillas until 1555, technically sharing the Crown. It was not until September 1517 that Charles arrived in his new kingdom because first the Netherlands had to be safeguarded from attack by offering concessions to the French in the Peace of Noyon. Cardinal Cisneros, the regent of Spain after Ferdinand's death, had been urging Charles to arrive as soon as possible because of widespread discontent in the country.

The nobility sought to take advantage of the power vacuum before Charles' arrival to re-establish the control they had lost under Ferdinand

and Isabella, and the towns were ready to fight to defend their privileges. Cisneros' attempt to raise a permanent army was defeated by both towns and grandees, who saw that it would have made the Crown militarily independent and Cisneros had to give way to prevent serious trouble.

The young, ugly and awkward king did not make a favourable first impression and his actions soon confirmed the Spaniards' worst fears. Cisneros was dismissed but he died before the letter could reach him. Worst of all, Burgndians were installed in key positions. To avoid breaking - his promise not to give offices to foreigners, Charles issued them with letters of naturalisation, a device which caused widespread resentment. The most glaring affront was the appointment of a seventeen year old Burgundian as the Archbishop of Toledo.

In spite of the tension, the Castilian Cortes (parliament) was persuaded to vote an exceptionally large servicio (tax) of 600 000 ducats payable over three years. Charles immediately left for Aragon where the more entrenched nature of the Cortes' privileges, the fueros, delayed his recognition as king and a grant of 200 000 ducats for eight months. In Catalonia, the process took a year and produced 100000 ducats. Before he could visit Valencia in 1519, Charles received news which meant he had to leave for Germany to ensure his succession as Holy Roman Emperor. Such a journey required ready cash.

To provide this money, the Castilian Cortes was summoned, in defiance of tradition, to the northern town of Santiago to vote a second servicio before the expiry of the first. The town of Toledo refused to send anyone and the instructions given to the deputies of Salamanca summed up the feelings of the Cortes: 'adjourn the Cortes. . . stop offices going to foreigners... do not agree to any servicio... the king's duty is to govern. . . by his presence, not by his absence.' It was only by the most intense pressure, and by adjourning the Cortes to La Coruna where Charles was preparing to set sail, that the court managed to secure a subsidy. The money was never collected and the alienation of Charles' Castilian subjects was now complete.

3. Revolt: Comuneros and Germania

Charles abandoned his Spanish kingdoms as they flared into revolt. The causes of the rebellion did not lie merely in his tactless handling of the Cortes or the appointment of foreigners. Resentment had been growing in the towns for years as a result of the Crown's failure to protect them against the attacks of the great aristocratic families. A myth developed of a golden age under the Catholic Kings and Charles was urged to 'act in everything like the Catholic lords, King Ferdinand and Queen Isabella'.

The accession of a foreign king and Emperor was unwelcome in three respects: he would be absent for much of the time; his empire was centred on distant north Europe; his advisers treated the Castilians 'as Indians'. Thus the Comunero movement which developed in the towns was essentially reactionary, united in a hatred of present conditions and groping after a previous, more satisfactory state. The demands issued in November 1520 asked that Charles return to Spain and marry soon; he should remove foreigners from his entourage; the Cortes was to be given a major role in government and to meet every three years; taxes and the expenses of the court should be reduced. None of these demands was revolutionary but even so Charles' position in Castile was soon in grave danger.

Following the lead of Toledo, riots broke out in most of the major towns of Castile. In Segovia the deputies who had voted for the new taxes were murdered. Royal authority broke down and the grandees, further angered by the appointment of Adrian of Utrecht as Regent despite Charles' promise to appoint no more foreigners did nothing to help the royal cause. The rebels found leadership in men such as Juan de Padilla, members of the lesser nobility of the towns, from whom the deputies to the Cortes were drawn.

A crisis was reached after the accidental burning of the great centre of Medma del Campo, which was blamed on government forces. In outrage, fourteen of the eighteen cities represented in the Cortes set up a Holy Junta and in September 1520 their forces seized Tordesiallas and Joanna, the legal Queen. If she had been persuaded to support the Comuneros in writing, it would have legitimised the rising and made the loss of Spain a real possibility. This was the climax of the rebellion but Joanna would sign nothing and the Comuneros could not agree on a common course of action. At this opportune moment, Adrian of Utrecht made some skillful concessions to win over the grandees. The Constable and Admiral of Castile were appointed co-regents; the collection of the servicio was to be suspended and no more foreigners would be appointed.

These concessions, combined with the increasingly radical nature of the revolt as it spread to the estates of the grandees and threatened their privileges, brought them over to the government's side. Old antagonisms between the towns and the nobility surfaced and at Villalar in April 1321, the Castilian nobles and their retainers destroyed the comunero army and executed Juan de Padilla and other leaders. This revolt was stopped just in time to prevent its exploitation by Francis I who had invaded Navarre. Castilians joined Aragonese in repelling the invader who was crushed at the battle of Pamplona in June 1521.

The revolt of the Comuneros was over but Charles could not take the credit. His inability to make quick decisions and the problems of ruling a country from the other end of Europe had brought his reign close to collapse. It was the transformation of the revolt into a social protest rather than a poiitica1 one which mobilised the forces of the nobility on his side. Despite this, Habsburg power was never seriously challenged in Castile again. The ceremony of swearing the fueros, liberties and privileges, at the start of each reign became a mere formality. The towns retained their privileges but the corregidores were re-established and the Cortes became little more than a tax-voting assembly. The deputies' salaries were paid from the taxes they voted and Charles refused to consider 'grievances' before supply (of taxation).

The nobles who had saved Charles were rewarded by being confirmed in their social position and privileges, above all in their exemption from axes, but they were increasingly excluded from the government of Spain. With a compliant Cortes, Charles could now afford a standing army and therefore he was less dependent on the power of the nobles.

The fragmented nature of the Spanish peninsula had been clearly illustrated in the revolt of the Comuneros not only by the failure of the Castilian towns to overcome their rivalry but also by the failure to link up with a major rebellion which broke out simultaneously in Valencia. This revolt of the Germania (brotherhood) never posed as great a threat to Charles because it was a class conflict which was dealt with by the nobility. The Germania had been set up to repel attacks by Barbary pirates but its leaders took the opportunity of a plague outbreak in Valencia in 1520 to seize control of the city and the surrounding countryside. The violence of the rebels ensured their eventual defeat at the hands of the nobility even though the rebellion spread across the whole kingdom and over into Majorca. The main forces of the Germania were defeated in October 1521, but resistance continued into 1523 and it was not until December 1524 that a general pardon was finally issued after the execution of hundreds of rebels.

The revolt was allowed to continue for so long because the government attached less importance to Valencia. A challenge to royal authority there lacked the force of a similar challenge in Castile and the nobles could therefore be left to control the revolt themselves.

The revolt of the Germania did not affect the privileges of the Aragonese. The nobility continued to exercise great power over their tenants and, in contrast to Castile, the Cortes maintained the right to discuss grievances before taxation, a privilege it was not worth the Crown contesting given the poverty of the eastern kingdoms. Aragon kept its liberty at a price, however. As J H Elliott saw, the history of Spain became in fact the history of Castile. Castilians became reconciled to the new, alien regime by the opportunities it opened up and by Charles' increasing attachment to his eventual homeland, while the Aragonese found themselves ever more isolated from affairs of state, especially after Charles' death.

4. The Government of Spain

Charles returned to Spain in July 1522 and remained there until 1529, his longest stay in the country during those seven years he married, remodelled the administration and underwent a decisive shift in outlook. When Charles left Spain again he was no longer a foreign monarch; he had adopted it as his spiritual home even if he was present there for only eight of his remaining 29 years. Spain had become the centre of his empire and the home of his family. In choosing Spain, Charles tied the interests of his dynasty to the Mediterranean and Atlantic, leaving the Austrian homeland of the Habsburgs, and therefore the Imperial crown, to his younger brother Ferdinand.

The other major feature of these years is the decisive relegation of Aragon to a secondary role. Charles continued the policy of Ferdinand in regarding Castile as 'the head of all the rest' because it was wealthier and more populous and also because it was easier to extract revenue from it.

Charles returned to a country that was still seething with discontent. It was vitally necessary to rebuild support for the monarchy rapidly because the treasury was in ruins: the Comuneros had taken the Crown's ordinary revenue for 1521—22 and the servicios had not been collected. Charles had to reduce popular hostility to his government and thus gain acceptance for his new taxes. A number of reforms were therefore adopted including the replacement of unpopular or corrupt officials The Cortes was allowed into partnership with the Crown. In return for taxes, it was responsible for handling revenue which provided opportunities for members of the Cortes to enrich themselves.

A partnership was also effected with the nobility. As the price for their exclusion from central government except on the king's terms, the nobility were allowed to govern the countryside with very little interference. Peace was brought to Spain but at considerable cost, with severe limitations on central policy and on the Crown's ability to make changes.

The Spanish empire had no institutions in common and no imperial bureaucracy. Any attempt at reform of the administration had to take account of the privileges of each territory and also the prolonged absence of the Emperor. But throughout Charles' huge empire there was a need for central direction and co-ordination of policies. Gattinara, the Imperial Chancellor, therefore developed the concilliar system of Ferdinand and Isabella by reforming the Council of Castile, creating the Councils of Finance and the Indies and remodelling the Council of War. Later, in 1555, a Council of Italy was created which completed the system. The councils were bureaucratic committees composed mainly of letrados (university trained lawyers) for the administration of royal policy. They communicated with the Emperor through a secretary who thereby acquired considerable power. The most important of these was Francisco de los Cobos, secretary of the Council of Finance, who was largely responsible for the administration of Spain in Charles' absence. An Andalucian of humble origins, he amassed a vast fortune but he was a reliable and efficient servant and as such enjoyed Charles' fullest confidence. Cobos was a rival of Gattinara's and this led to a decline in the latter's influence from about 1527. After Gattinara's death, Charles became his own Chancellor with Cobos responsible for Spanish and Mediterranean affairs and Nicholas Perrenot, Lord of Granvelle, his leading adviser on the Netherlands and the empire.

The secretaries acted as filters for incoming correspondence and decided whether a dispatch should go direct to the Emperor or first to the appropriate council for discussion. The system also gave council members, and especially the secretaries, enormous patronage as they controlled access to the Emperor. Corruption was rife and the bureaucracy grew to parasitic proportions. Although it worked adequately in ordinary circumstances the conciliar system found it hard to respond to crises. This is clearly seen in the council of Finance.

5. Finance

The Council of Finance was created in 1523 to supervise and control all income and expenditures and to establish regular and efficient means of raising money. In fact the enormous scale of Charles' commitments meant that all the Council could do was to stave off bankruptcy by a series of desperate measures, such as the sale of offices or the seizure of private shipments of bullion. The government of each of Charles' territories was in theory self-supporting but in practice by the end of the reign several, such as the German territories, were reliant upon the subsidies of other areas. In addition, there were the constant wars against France and the Turks which were an impossible burden (as Phillip II's bankruptcy in 1557 was to show).

Castile came to play an increasingly vital role in the financing of the empire, not because it was particularly rich, rather the reverse, but because of the ease with which money could be extracted from it once the Cortes of Castile had been humbled. The influx of bullion from the New World, although not significant until the end of the reign, was channelled through Castile and this was a readily obtainable source of wealth. For this reason, above all, Castile became the centre of Charles' empire and the most frequently tapped supply of funds. The results for Castile itself were not entirely favourable.

Initially Charles relied most heavily on the Netherlands and Italy for money as these were the wealthiest parts of his empire. However the scale of the tax demands placed upon them led to revolt in Ghent in 1539 and to the viceroy of Naples complaining that further claims would be 'to squeeze juice from a stone.' In 1540 Charles wrote to his brother, Ferdinand, 'I cannot be sustained except by my realms of Spain', and in effect this meant Castile, which henceforth bore the brunt of imperial expenditure. This was done with the agreement of the nobility as they were exempt from taxation. The Cortes invariably voted the huge sums demanded of them because they were unaffected. The unevenness of the tax burden was recognised by the rulers. In 1545 Philip wrote to his father: 'The common people who have to pay the servicios are reduced to such distress and misery that many of them walk naked'. Charles had made an attempt to spread the distribution of taxes more widely in 1538 when he summoned the nobility and clergy to attend the Cortes and proposed the introduction of a new tax on foodstuffs, the sisa, which would be payable by all. The nobility refused to abandon their tax-free status and as a result were never again summoned to the Cortes, which found itself powerless to refuse the increasingly arbitrary demands of the Crown. The nobles' financial privilege had been bought at the expense of their political influence over government policy.

Instead Charles relied more heavily on servicios, non-noble taxes, and on a number of more dubious expedients such as the sale of juros, government bonds which carried a fixed annual interest and which meant mortgaging future revenues for present gain. He also used the services of foreign bankers whose interest rates climbed steeply as the reignprogressed. To pay this interest, specific items of revenue were assigned to each debt and thus it was that by 1554 all revenue had been anticipated (earmarked for debt repayment) up to 1560. Castile's resources were swallowed up to meet expenses, most of which had little to do with Spanish interests.

6. The Economy

Charles presided over the start of Spain's 'golden age' when it became the most powerful state in Europe with an admired and feared army, a vigorous cultural life and an expanding overseas empire that produced unimagined wealth. But he has also been criticised by historians such as Koenigsberger for distorting the Spanish economy and failing to provide the right circumstances for growth with the result that eventually Spain became an economic backwater from which it is still struggling to emerge. His over-riding need for money made it impossible for Charles to develop a coherent economic strategy. The opportunities afforded by the opening up of the New World ought to have given Spanish, and especially Castilian, trade and industry a great stimulus. In fact it proved totally unable to cope with the demands of the colonists and it was foreign merchants who benefited the most.

There was little understanding of economic forces and at one stage Charles agreed to a ban on all exports of cloth except to the Indies in an effort to keep domestic prices down. That caused such a depression in the textile industry the ban had to be lifted after five years.

The reasons for the high prices which prompted the export ban are uncertain, but it has been claimed that the influx of bullion was partly responsible. Bullion helped to finance Charles' wars and to provide an extravagant lifestyle for the nobles but it was not used for investment in industry and provided no lasting benefit to the economy. Heay taxation discouraged industrial investment, which was despised, and the greatest financial return was to be obtained by buying juros. It was the pressing demands of warfare that led to the failure to develop an economy in the New World to compliment Castile's, or to build up the Castilian economy for future benefit. Money was always required immediately and this effectively prevented any long-term strategy.

Some parts of the Spanish economy did flourish in Charles' reign. Seville and its hinterland enjoyed the fruits that a monopoly of the Atlantic trade gave them; the ironworks of the Basque region flourished; ceramics, leather and silk were all in demand. However, Spanish agriculture was neglected and backward. Too much emphasis was placed on the rearing of sheep, encouraged by the government because of the taxes it produced, but this meant that, with an expanding home market as well as the Indies, Castile was regularly importing wheat by 1560. Increased demand led to higher prices and the consequence of the empire for the ordinary Spaniard was a decline in living standards.

In general it can be said that opportunities were missed to put the Spanish economy on a sound footing that would enable it to meet the demands of imperialism. That Spain managed to maintain an illusion of strength as Europe's greatest power until 1660 says more for the long-suffering of the ordinary people than it does for the inherent strength of the economy. Decline, when it became evident, was swift and almost irreversible.

With hindsight, it is easy to see Charles' handling of the Spanish economy as his greatest failure. Henry Kamen points out how other countries profited from Spain's failures. Armaments were imported from Italy and textiles from England to provide for Spanish colonists' needs. The Cortes of Valladolid complained in 1548: 'Spain has become an Indies for the foreigner'. And by the seventeenth century five-sixths of the trade from Cadiz was not in the hands of Spaniards. In criticising Charles' lack of imagination, however, we must bear in mind the very imperfect understanding of economic forces and his desperate need for ready cash. Investment in industrial enterprises was a risky business with a slow and uncertain return. On the other hand, bullion was very acceptable to foreign financiers who would lend large sums on the security of future shipments. As is often the case with governments, short-term expediency triumphed over long-term planning.

The 1520s and 1530s saw both the circumnavigation of the world by Magellan's expedition and the conquest of Mexico and Peru by Cortés and Pizarro. For the Indians the effect of conquest was devastating: the cruelty of the Spaniards, their diseases and their labour demands combined to reduce the native population of Mexico from about 25.2 million in 1518 to 2.65 million in 1568. The belated recognition by the government that the labour force was being destroyed led to the decision to import black slaves from Africa, with incalculable results. It also led to the passing of the New Laws in 1542 which freed, at least in law, all Indian slaves in the New World and set up an organised system of audiencias (courts) and officials under a viceroy. Despite its imperfections, this system worked reasonably well and can justifiably be seen as one of Charles' successes.

Spain achieved its greatest glory under Charles and his descendants. For 150 years the rest of Europe feared and respected its power. The foundations of this power were, however, less solid than they appeared. The enormous scale of Charles V's commitments, above all the struggle in Germany and Eastern Europe, led to a distortion of the Spanish economy for reasons which had no connection with Spain. The country was saddled with an intolerable burden of debt which led to successive bankruptcies in future decades. Specifically Spanish interests, above all in the Mediterranean, were neglected for problems in the rest of the monarchia, so that Spain's glory was also her weakness. The privileges of empire could not be divorced from the burdens.

7. Charles' Empire: The Monarchia

The seven years that Charles spent in Spain from 1522—29 was the most settled period of his reign. Charles declared, 'My life has been one long journey'. One quarter of the days of his reign were spent in travelling at a time when this was often extremely hazardous. On his first journey from the Netherlands to Spain, apart from long delays and a storm which forced him to land on an inhospitable part of the Spanish coast, the ship carrying his horses caught fire and all 160 on board were lost.

This constant travel was necessary because of the fragmented nature of Charles' empire. Because it had no centre and no one territory took precedence over another, at least in theory, Charles continued to rule each part as if he were present in person. To maintain this fiction, he had to make an appearance as often as possible, so Charles visited Germany nine times, Spain six times, the Netherlands on ten occasions and Italy on seven. Despite this level of activity, Charles was only able to maintain his system of government through the good offices of his family who acted as his regents. Only Italy and the Indies had to make do with non-royal viceroys. The Netherlands were well governed by first Margaret of Austria and then Mary of Hungary, Charles' sister. Ferdinand was in charge of the

Empire in the absence of Charles, and later Philip his son ruled Spain. The use of royal governors helped to suppress unrest but even so there was widespread dissatisfaction in most areas over Charles' continual absences, and some problems only he could solve. Thus the German Protestants were able to flourish until Charles could deal with them himself.

One reason for the desire to have Charles present was that he controlled all patronage and the benefits of advancement it could bring. This could hamper the regents as they were unable to buy support for a royal party. Charles insisted on taking all major decisions himself despite the inefficiency this led to, but no central administration was created nor was a unified tax system developed. The only central institutions were the councils which travelled with Charles and this is why the role of secretary was so important.

Gattinara had a vision of a true union of all Charles' territories, hoping that he would eventually be the legislator of the whole world, but nothing came of this idea. Gattinara himself was the only link between the territories (apart from Charles) because he exercised jurisdiction over all of them and presided over all councils. He saw Italy as the centre of Charles' empire and the struggle for Milan as therefore of the first importance. If Charles could win Italy and the friendship of the Pope, he would be able to dominate Europe. Gattinara died in 1530 at an auspicious moment when it seemed as if his dream was realised. Charles did not appoint another chancellor, taking on the duties himself, but he had absorbed much of Gattinara's outlook.

However, the concept of a universal empire had to come to terms with political realities. The Holy Roman Empire from which Charles derived his prestigious title was where he in fact enjoyed least power. Ihe sizç of the monarchia and the threat it posed to other states meant that Charles was eqgaged in a constant struggle with hostile forces and his twin aims of fighting the Infidel and eradicating heresy would remain unrealised. Charles drew his main strength from Spain and the Netherlands. The rest of his territories in Europe were a drain on his resources because of the conflicts they were involved in, either with France, the Turks or the Protestants.

8. The Netherlands

Charles' ancestral home, the Netherlands, where his reign began and ended, provided crucial resources for the Emperor's wars in the first part of his reign. Charles made relatively frequent, but brief, visits to the Netherlands (ten visits totalling twelve years) and he relied heavily on the capable services of his aunt, Margaret of Austria, and sister, Mary of Hungary.

The Netherlands were the most urbanised part of Europe. They were the richest of Charles' territories with a flourishing cloth industry and enterprising merchants. For many years Charles was dependent on the subsidies they granted him. In 1559 Soriano, the Venetian ambassador, wrote 'These lands are the treasuries of the King of Spain, his mines and his Indies, they have financed the enterprises of the Emperor for so many years in the wars of France, Italy and Germany.' Already, however, this was no longer true. As in Spain, Charles taxed his subjects until they would pay no more. In so doing he provoked serious opposition, especially in Ghent, and, more seriously, stirred up hostility to the notion of foreign rule. This was kept in check during his reign because of his personal popularity as a Burgundian, but it surfaced with great vigour when his son, a complete Spaniard, took over. The Low Countries resented the fact that the money they voted was not always spent in their interests. In particular, they disliked the war with France.

Charles was eager to bring the provinces of the Netherlands into a closer union and provide them with a more efficient and centralised government. Each province had its own Estates (parliament) and this made effective control more difficult. In 1531 the Council of State set up a Council of Finance to co-ordinate the collection of taxes, and a High Court of Appeal. Both were strongly opposed, as was a plan in 1534 to create a standing army paid for by each province, for if we accept the proposal we shall undoubtedly be more united, but we shall be dealt with in the manner of France' i.e. with a loss of local liberties (Spain and Germany also resisted similar proposals for the same reason).

Charles realised that to insist on reforms might jeopardise his sources of revenue and therefore refrained from pushing his claims too far. He was forced to concede the redress of grievances before supply and to watch every demand for money being haggled over and whittled down. The Provincial Estates were even allowed to build up their own administrative machinery to control the collection and expenditure of the taxes they voted. The government derived one major advantage from its failure to centralise and that was the continuing localism of the Estates. Whilst there was no political unity, there would be no concerted opposition to challenge the position of royal authority.

This became increasingly important as the government increased its demands for money against a steadily rising tide of, discontent. War disrupted trade and was therefore damaging to the, economy and the Netherlands were very vulnerable to attacks from France, so there were constant demands for peace. These were ignored by Charles and as a result there were riots in Bois-le-Duc in 1525, Brussels in 1532 and in 1537 Ghrles' birthplace Ghent began a tax strike that had flared into rebellion by 1539.

Ghent was a city in decline and the demands for subsidies in the French war of 1537 had been too much. The whole of Flanders was equally dissatisfied but the revolt failed to become general because the guilds setup a democratic dictatorship and terrorised the government's supporters in the upper classes, thus frightening potential leaders in other areas. Charles took the revolt seriously enough to come in person in 1540 to crush it. Ghent lost its charter, was forced to pay a heavy fine, a quarter of the town was pulled down to make a fortress and representatives of all classes had to beg pardon barefoot and on their knees. Such harsh punishment was intended to deter potential imitators, and the excessive tax demands continued. The Netherlands claimed that in five years they had given Charles extraordinary grants of eight million ducats, yet he still left his son Philip with a sizeable debt.

In religion, Charles acted with severity. The laws against heresy ('Placaten' became increasingly harsh throughout the reign although already Lutherans were being burnt in 1523. Despite this, Lutheran and radical preachers found a ready audience among the artisans of the towns and heresy continued to spread and flourish.

Superficially, Charles' reign was successful in the Netherlands. Certainly he extended its territory by annexing Tournai (1521) and Cambrai (1543) from the French and creating six northern provinces by the defeat in 1543 of William, Duke of Cleves, the successor to Charles of Egmont, Duke of Guelders. The Netherlands thus became a coherent at least in geographical terms. However, there was no political union and little sense of a common identity as the course of the Revolt of the Netherlands in the latter half of the century was to show. Charles detached the Netherlands from the Empire, with which it had little in common, and created the prospect of a powerful North Sea empire by the marriage of Philip to Mary Tudor in 1554. The frustration of this hope by Mary's childless death in 1558 left the Netherlands as an isolated outpost of a Spanish empire that was firmly centred on the Mediterranean. In such a context, with a foreign king as ruler, the latent discontent which had scarcely been suppressed under Charles would surface with explosive force that would require great tact to manage. Charles' legacy to Philip in the Netherlands was potentially a powder keg.

9. Habsburg—Valois Rivalry 1521—29

Any consideration of a map of Europe in 1520 will show that one power would be constantly threatened by the encircling wings of Charles V's empire. This power was France, which engaged in a series of wars against Charles, mainly in Italy, to prevent his domination of the peninsula and the completion of the circle which Charles' capture of Milan would represent. Charles had begun his reign at a disadvantage compared to the already victorious Francis I. He was forced to sign the Treaty of Noyon (1516) in order to ensure French neutrality while he went to Spain to claim his inheritance. This involved, amongst other humiliating clauses, paying France an annual tribute of 100000 ducats. Three years later, however, the tables were turned when Charles became Holy Roman Emperor and immediately took precedence over his rival.

This rivalry with Francis I was at the heart of Charles' problem as Emperor. Francis would never accept his claim to leadership of Christendom, arid French interference in Italy and support for the Pope could prevent Charles from dominating the Papacy and securing the alliance he hoped for, which would be essential if he was to make his dream of leadership a reality. The threat to Francis was more of a psychological one than a reality. Charles had no desire to conquer France, and no hope of doing so. However, Francis had to maintain his prestige by constantly diverting Charles from problems in the Empire and against the Turks, by forcing him to engage in costly wars over Italy.

Northern Italy, and specifically Milan, was crucial to Charles because it provided a route from Spain to Austria along which troops could pass when necessary. It was also important to have a safe overland route to the Netherlands. Milan was the key to this too. (The 'Spanish Road' was to increase in importance under Philip II.) If Charles lost control of Milan to France, the different elements of his empire would be isolated and effective action would become extremely difficult. The only alternative route to the Netherlands was by sea, which was also vulnerable to the French, and it therefore became important to secure the co-operation of England which was forthcoming in the early 1520s at least.

Not only was Charles a threat to Francis but also the reverse was true. Charles had the difficulty of co-ordinating men and money from scattered territories, with France eager to exploit any weakness in the chain. Meanwhile, France as a unitary state did not experience the same logistical problems and could strike at whichever part of the empire seemed vulnerable. Charles was a man of integrity and he found the unscrupulous Francis very hard to deal with, especially when the latter allied with the great enemy of Christendom, the Ottoman Empire.

There were also other irritants to drive the two sides apart. Italy had been a battleground since the fifteenth century and only domination by one side would end the conflict there. Charles wished to regain Burgundy, the ancestral home of his dynasty, annexed by France in 1477. Similarly, the incorporation of Navarre into Castile was not recognised by France. These old disputes could be revived whenever circumstances seemed appropriate (so France tried to take advantage of the revolt of the Comuneros by reasserting claims to Navarre).

Ultimately, Francis I could not tolerate Charles' claim to dominance The latter might protest, as he did in 1536, 'There are those who say that I wish to rule the world, but both my thoughts and my deeds demonstrate the contrary'. But this was hardly enough to dissuade Francis from plotting the downfall of his great rival.

The effect upon Charles' policies was immediately apparent. Decisive action against the emergent German Protestantism had to be postponed and, not for the last time, the internal needs of Charles' empire were sacrificed to the struggle against 'the most Christian' King of France.

Trouble flared up in 1521; to distract Charles from interference in Italy, French troops invaded the Netherlands and Navarre. Both campaigns went badly. Charles seized Tournai, the Spanish united against the French threat and, in Italy, Imperial troops took Milan, defeating a Franco-Swiss army at Bicocca in 1522. Charles had also secured alliance with the Pope and England for a joint attack on France. When Adrian of Utrecht succeeded Leo X as Pope in January 1522, it looked as if Gattinara's two conditions for the success of Charles as Emperor—the domination of Italy and alliance with Rome—had been fulfilled.

It was to be a short lived illusion. Adrian died in 1523 and a combined attack upon France by Charles and Henry VIII was a miserable failure. In 1524, Francis I invaded Italy in person and recaptured Milan, and the new Pope, Clement VII, abandoned the Imperial side. Charles gloomily committed his thoughts to paper:

> 'I cannot support my army let alone increase it, if that should be necessary . . . My friends have forsaken me in my evil hour; all are equally determined to prevent me from growing more powerful and to keep me in my present distressed state. . . A

battle in which I shall be either victorious or wholly defeated cannot be postponed for much longer...'

The decisive battle in fact came as Charles wrote. Outside the city of Pavia on February 24 1525 (Charles' twenty-fifth birthday), Francis I was captured and his army suffered a crushing defeat. This unexpected victory did not bring Charles much advantage: it increased Italian fears of Habsburg power and led to a split with Henry VIII. Charles was also determined to win back the old Burgundian lands, an impossible condition for Francis to fulfil and one which the French nation would probably have resisted. As a result, negotiations with the royal prisoner, who was taken to Madrid, made no progress. Meanwhile the Regent of France, Francis' mother Louise of Savoy, was making alliances with Italian cities, Henry VIII and the Turks. Eventually the stalemate was broken. Francis made a secret vow to declare his promises null and void on his return to France and he was then ready to sign the Treaty of Madrid in January 1526. This bound him to seek the permission of the Estates General for the return of Burgundy to Charles; to renounce claims to territories held by Charles in Italy and the Netherlands; to reinstate Bourbon; to marry Charles' sister, Eleanor, and to join a crusade against the Turks.

Charles had won a battle but he had not won the war and the treaty brought Charles nothing. The holding hostage of the two eldest French princes was not enough to prevent Francis I from denouncing the treaty and forming the League of Cognac. Francis then made an alliance with Suleiman I, the Ottoman Emperor, which contributed to the latter's victory at Mohacs by diverting possible aid that Charles might have given to the Hungarians.

The Turks now directly threatened the hereditary Habsburg lands in Austria but, for Charles, war against France took priority and he continued to demand troops for Italy from his brother Ferdinand, a request which was met but which strained the younger man's loyalty. In Germany, the Lutherans were offered an amnesty in return for their support of the Empire and to relieve the pressure on Ferdinand. As before, the struggle against France in Italy took precedence over other concerns.

Charles' troops in Italy now took matters into their own hands. They had been short of money since Pavia and the idea grew at the end of 1526 that the Pope was to blame for all their distress. In 1527 the starving, leaderless soldiers moved inexorably south and sacked Rome in an orgy of looting and destruction that appalled the rest of Europe. Although unintended by Charles, he could hardly ignore the imprisonment of the Pope, but passed the summer in a state of indecision while his enemies seized the upper hand.

The problem for Charles was that he regarded alliance with the Pope as his right, but the popes were unreliable and unco-operative. As with Francis I, however, Charles could not see how to exploit the fact that he held the Pope prisoner. In 1528 it seemed as if Imperial troops might be pushed out of Italy altogether. Things were going badly in the north, while Naples was besieged on land by the French and blockaded at sea by the Genoese. This desperate situation was transformed by the sudden defection of the Genoese naval commander, Andrea Doria, to Charles side because of insensitive French treatment, This event was crucial both for Habsburg control of Italy and in the coming struggle for the Mediterranean with the Turks. Communications between Italy and Spain were safeguarded and Charles came to rely increasingly on Genoese money and soldiers.

In the short term the Genoese alliance saved Naples and, after defeat at Landriano the following year, Francis I was ready to make peace Charles made peace first with the Pope in the Treaty of Barcelona Clement recognised Charles as ruler of Naples, granted him the cruza (a Spanish tax paid for a Bull of Indulgence granted every three years and agreed to crown him Emperor. In return, Charles promised to uphold the rights of the Pope's relatives, the Medici, in Florence. The Treaty of Cambrai (1529) signed with France repeated the Treaty of Madrid without the claim to Burgundy.

10. From Victory to Defeat 1530-59

Charles was now at the height of his power he had secured a very favourable treaty with France and in 1530 he was crowned Holy Roman Emperor by the Pope in great splendour at Bologna. Attention could thus be given to the other pressing problems of his reign, the Turks and the Lutherans. Francis I recognised the futility of direct action against Charles but continued to intrigue with his enemies, making alliance with the Duke of Cleves, Henry VIII, Suleiman and the Pope (whose niece, Catherine de Medici, married Francis' son, Henry).

The chance to re-open the war came when Francesco Sforza, Duke of Milan, died childless in 1535. As a preliminary to claiming Milan, Francis marched into Savoy, the gateway to Italy, in 1536 and occupied Turin. This was an act of pure aggression caused by the fear of direct Habsburg rule in Milan and enabled Charles to pose convincingly as the responsible protector of Christendom, but even so he was unable to win the active support of the Pope (Paul III since 1534) and had to be content with his neutrality.

The war went badly for Charles who made the mistake of attacking France itself, but the French were also unable to make headway and, after a year's inconclusive fighting, the Pope negotiated a ten year truce at Nice (1538). This solved nothing; Francis remained in possession of Savoy and Piedmont, but it allowed Charles to pursue grandiose dreams of a crusade against the Turks while on a more mundane level it gave his hard-pressed treasury some relief, although in Castile all revenue was anticipated up to 1540.

The truce was not destined to last ten years. Francis was ready to use any pretext to resume the conflict and was eager to take advantage of Charles' weakness after the failure in Algiers. 'The excuse was the murder of two French envoys in Milan. Francis I declared war in July 1542. Fighting took place on three fronts, in Milan, the Pyrenees and the Netherlands. Only the latter was under real threat. The French were in alliance with the Duke of Cleves who had a claim to Guelderland and large parts of the Netherlands were devastated. However Francis lost support by his open alliance during this war with the Turks, the enemies of Christendom, and

Charles had been able to increase his revenues by the dowry for the Portuguese Infanta who married his son Philip. Charles left Spain for the last time as ruling monarch and crushed the Duke of Cleves before winning Cambrai from the French. The unification of the Netherlands was now complete with the encroaching territories of Guelderland, Utrecht and Cambrai all under Charles' control.

Charles now took the offensive and invaded France, causing panic in Paris while Henry VIII, his ally, captured Boulogne. Francis I was forced to come to terms and in the Peace of Crépy, 1544, all conquests made since 1538 were restored. France agreed to support the calling of a General Council of the Church and to help against the Turks and the German Protestants. The Duke of Orleans was to marry either Charles' daughter or his niece who would receive the Netherlands or Milan as a dowry. This came to nothing because the Duke died in 1545, 'just in time' as Charles admitted in his memoirs.

In 1547 Francis I died, shortly before Charles' great triumph at Muhlberg. It looked as if the Habsburg—Valois struggle had been decided in favour of the former. Charles had no equal in Europe and the stranglehold on France was tighter than ever; yet within six years Charles was a broken man, seeking only to escape from the trials of the world.

Francis I was succeeded by Henry II whose anti-Habsburg feelings had been encouraged by his years as a captive in Spain. He abandoned the struggle in Italy in order to concentrate on Charles' weakest spot by allying with the German Protestants. In the Treaty of Chambord of 1552, the Protestants agreed Henry should have the key Rhine bishoprics of Metz, Tours and Verdun in return for his support in the war against Charles. After coming to terms with the Protestants, which he found deeply humiliating, Charles made a valiant but unsuccessful attempt to recapture Metz, which, as he wrote to his sister Mary, gave the French 'a clear road to the Rhine and so they will be able to cut off my communications from South Germany to the Netherlands and Franche Comté.'

His failure at Metz in 1553, coupled with the victory of the Protestants, convinced Charles that God had deserted him and he began to seek the best way to abdicate. The siege of Metz had been ruinously expensive (it had cost two million ducats) and money could no longer be raised, even at interest rates of nearly 50 percent. Charles decided a younger man must tackle the problems and his reign ended with the final phase of the conflict with France unresolved.

Charles' son, Philip II, began his reign with a five year truce with France. This lasted barely a year before Pope Paul IV, who nursed a fanatical hatred of the Habsburgs, re-opened the conflict by trying to oust Philip from Naples, and summoning the French to his aid. Fighting resumed on all fronts and the Spanish won a major victory at San Quentin but they were unable to follow this up because of lack of funds. Both Philip II and Henry II were forced into bankruptcy in 1557 and exhaustion prompted both sides to peace. Two factors combined to improve the prospects of a lasting peace. The break-up of Charles V's inheritance removed the irritant of encirclement from France, and the death of Philip's wife, Mary Tudor, in November 1558 broke the Spanish—English alliance which was so dangerous to France.

The Peace of Câteau-Cambrésis (1559) was a triumph for Charles V's southern struggles against the French. Italy, with the exception of Venice, became almost a Spanish province. Spanish dominance in the peninsula was secured and with it the 'Spanish Road' to the Netherlands. All France retained were five fortresses in Savoy. In the north, the advantage was with the French. Henry II retained Metz, Toulon and Verdun and did not restore Calais to the English, while Philip withdrew from occupied towns in northern France. Many of the provisions of the treaty lasted for a century as France was riven by forty years of internal strife, allowing Spain unchallenged dominance of western Europe.

11. The Struggle with the Ottomans

For centuries Christendom and Islam had co-existed with uneasy relations on the frontiers. Islam had come closest in Spain, where the Moors were only finally defeated in Granada in 1492. Then the main threat came from the Barbary pirates and their raids on shipping and the coast. But this was no more than an irritant for a long time. This secure state was shattered by the emergence of the aggressive Ottoman Empire which was committed to conquest and expansion. The fall of Constantinople in 1453 opened the way to the Mediterranean and in 1522 Rhodes fell—the last bastion of Christian power, except for Cyprus, in the eastern half of the sea. The previous year had seen the conquest of Belgrade, exposing the Danube, a route that would take the Turks deep into Europe and enable them to threaten Vienna, at the heart of the hereditary Habsburg lands.

Thus, within a few years of assuming power, Charles V was faced with the task of preventing further incursions by the Turks. He was in the front line of any attack and inevitably the activities of the Sultan were a cause of constant concern. Ferdinand bore the major responsibility for defending central Europe, although Charles assisted him when he could; it was in the Mediterranean that Charles was more closely involved. One of his most cherished wishes was to lead a crusade against the Turks, but the politics of Christendom never allowed this. Instead, Charles was denied the opportunity to take decisive action against the Turks in his home territory of the western Mediterranean by the scale of his commitments elsewhere. The reverse was also true. The pressure of the Turks on his eastern flank prevented harsh measures against the German Protestants until it was too late.

For Charles' Spanish subjects in the south, firm action against the Turks was essential if they were not to be in continual fear of attack from Barbary pirates who became immeasurably more threatening in alliance with the Turks and with the possibility of internal revolt by the Moriscos. In 1516, the pirate Barbarossa had established himself in Algiers and become a vassal of the Sultan. In 1532 he became grand admiral of the entire Turkish fleet. This exposed the coasts of Italy and Spain, which suffered constant raids, and seriously threatened Charles' communications. This was especially serious in Sicily which acted as a granary for other parts of the empire. Charles was unable to take action against Barbarossa until the l530s when he had the help of the Genoese.

There was no Spanish fleet which could compare with that of the Turks and no effort was made to build one. However, when Charles arrived back in Spain in 1533 after an absence of four years, he was anxious to fulfil his religious mission and to please his Spanish subjects by striking a blow at the Turks.

This became more urgent after 1534 when Barbarossa made a daring attack on Italy that brought him close to Rome, and on his return captured Tunis. This was too serious to he ignored and Charles decided to lead in person an expedition to conquer Tunis, the gateway to the western Mediterranean, thus winning glory for himself as well as protecting the western Mediterranean. La Goletta and Tunis were taken in 1535 and 85 of Barbarossa's galleys—the bulk of his fleet—were captured. Although spectacular, the victory did not alter the balance of power. Barbarossa escaped to Algiers and within a few weeks had organised an attack on Minorca. Charles lacked the naval strength to follow up his acclaimed triumph and in 1536 the French entered into open alliance with the Sultan, which opened French ports to his ships.

War with France (1536—38) prevented a continuation of the Mediterranean campaign until after the Truce of Nice (see page 195). Charles then arranged an alliance with the Venetians and the Pope but distrust between these allies led to their defeat by the Turks at the Battle of Prevesa off the Greek coast in 1538. The Venetians made a separate peace with the Turks and without their galleys it was impossible for the western alliance to offer effective resistance to the Turkish fleet. Charles decided to strike at the heart of Barbarossa's power—Algiers. He regarded his mission as a Holy War and again led his troops in person. Unfortunately the campaign in 1541, which started out too late in the year, was a disaster. One hundred and fifty ships were lost in a storm and Charles was forced to retreat with his army almost intact, partly because his own captivity or death could not be risked. This was a great blow to his reputation and put an end to serious moves against the Turks in the Mediterranean.

In 1543—44 the Turkish fleet wintered in Toulon and Christian slaves were sold in the market. In 1551 Tripoli was taken with ease by the new leader of the Turkish fleet, Dragut, providing another useful link in the chain with Algiers. Alarmed by the threat to Sicily, Charles removed Spanish and Italian troops from Wurttemberg, thus directly encouraging the German rebellion of 1552. What saved the western Mediterranean from complete Turkish domination was its distance from Turkey, the internal dynastic problems of Suleiman, and war against Persia. Charles V and Suleiman I faced similar problems. Their empires were too big to make concerted action in one area a possibility for long. Both linked up with the other's enemies but in the end the empires were too far apart for a decisive confrontation between them. Charles had dreamed of a crusade against Constantinople. Instead he had been unable to safeguard even his own territories.

The naval power of the Turks was worrying but posed a less serious threat than the huge armies which Suleiman could muster for attack on central Europe. While German attention was focused on the Diet of Worms in 1521, Suleiman was capturing Belgrade and thus exposing Hungary to his attacks. The challenge was delayed for four years, but in 1526 he returned in force and wiped out the Hungarian army, together with its king, Louis II, at the battle of Mohacs. As brother-in-law to the childless Louis, Ferdinand claimed the crowns of Bohemia and Hungary despite the opposition of the powerful noble John Zapolyai who wanted the throne himself. Zapolyai won the support of Suleiman by swearing allegiance to him, presenting Ferdinand with a double threat. In 1529, the most serious attack on Habsburg power was launched. Vienna was besieged for three weeks until the onset of autumn forced the Turks to withdraw. It was the immense distances involved which saved the Habsburg lands because the campaigning season was eight to ten weeks kng. The further the Ottomans penetrated into enemy territory, the hwigcr were their lines of communication: the campaigning season hecame progressively shorter and the likelihood of further conquest rc remote. Charles also made diplomatic contact with the Shah of Persia as a way of pressurising their common enemy.

In 1529, Ferdinand's pleas for aid had been largely ignored as Charles concentrated on securing his coronation before tackling the German problem. By 1532, when there was news of the approach of another large Turkish army, he was ready to show more positive support. A large army as assembled which confronted the 'Turks at Guns and forced them to retreat. The advantage was not followed up because the German troops refused to cross the frontier into Hungary. This failure was deeply disappointing to Ferdinand: inevitably his interests lay in central Europe and his devotion to Charles' wishes was often strained as the latter's attention was heavily concentrated on the western Mediterranean. For his part, Charles had not welcomed Ferdinand's election as King of Bohemia and Hungary because of increased conflict with the Turks and he was most concerned to ensure peace on his eastern flank so he would be able to deal with other matters. Ferdinand's negotiations with Suleiman were therefore not unwelcome and the latter part of the reign saw a diminution of the Turkish threat, with the exception of the early 1540s when a fully Turkish administration was established in eastern Hungary. Uneasy co-existence could bring trouble. As late as 1683 the Turks were besieging Vienna. The problem was contained in the sixteenth century, not solved. The most serious effect of Turkish activity in central Europe was seen in Germany. Distraction by the Infidel was to cost Charles dear in his dealings with the heretic Lutherans.

12. The Holy Roman Empire and the Protestant Threat

Charles was unanimously elected Holy Roman Emperor in 1519 in succession to his grandfather Maximilian. The title remained in the Habsburg family until it died out and therefore it is easy to regard Charles' election as a foregone conclusion. This was not the case. The seven electors (Cologne, Mainz, Trier, Bohemia, the Palatinate, Brandenburg and Saxony) guarded their independence and the issue was in doubt to the end. The electors were persuaded to choose Charles by a combination of factors: he was prepared to spend most money in bribes—the election cost him nearly one million gold gulden; the Pope supported his main rival,

Francis I, and Charles was unlikely to be able to interfere too much with the privileges of the princes given the scattered nature of his territories. Thus Charles became the pre-eminent ruler in Christendom. It was a dubious honour. The Empire entailed far more responsibilities than privileges since the title brought with it no actual power, only prestige, and it was in the Empire that Charles was to be defeated.

Germany was the largest nation in Europe, with great resources. However it was impossible to use these for common political objectives because of its internal disunity. There were more than 2500 different authorities, mainly knights but also great princes, Church leaders and cities, which acknowledged no overlord except the Emperor. The Emperor was limited by the Diet which represented the electors, the princes and the free Imperial cities. Without the co-operation of the Diet, the Emperor was powerless unless he could muster troops of his own to enforce his will—this was very seldom possible and even then he relied on the support of at least some of the Diet's members. In the early sixteenth century, both Maximilian and Charles made attempts to reform the Empire to make it a more coherent unit but these plans came to little, mainly because the princes were unwilling to surrender any of their power. There was a general desire for a united Germany in theory, but not at the expense of anyone's privileges. The development of a religious split in the Empire made an already difficult situation impossible for its ruler.

Charles was deeply hurt by the appearance of heresy within his territories and pledged himself in 1521 to its eradication: 'To settle this matter, I am determined to use my kingdoms and dominions, my friends, my body, my blood, my life and my soul'. Unfortunately for him, it was politically expedient for many of the princes to adopt Lutheranism and without their active support, Charles could do little. The crucial middle years of the 1520s were devoted to settling Spain and by the time Charles turned his full attention back to the Empire, the Lutherans had established themselves too firmly to be easily dealt with. Charles' desire to give them a fair hearing and win them back by compromise through the action of a General Council also played into the Protestants' hands because it gave them over twenty years to build up their strength before an open confrontation took place.

Charles returned to Germany in 1530 for the Diet of Augsburg, fresh from his coronation as Emperor by the Pope and at the peak of his power. Peace had been secured with France and he was now anxious to settle the religious problem so that a united Empire could face the Turkish threat. It was not to be so simple. The Catholic majority in the Diet was not prepared to use force against the Protestants until a General Council of the Church had met, something Pope Clement VII was resolutely opposed to. Despite a desire for compromise on both sides, the conciliatory Augsburg Confession was too much for Charles to accept. When the Protestants withdrew from the Diet, it was decided to return to the Edict of Worms after a delay of six months. In response, the Protestants formed the Schmalkaldic League in 1531.

Further action against the Protestants was postponed by the approach of a huge army under Suleiman. A religious truce meant that all the Estates sent help to Charles which enabled him to halt the Turks at Guns. This was the first of a series of temporary truces granted to the Protestants as Charles required all his strength for the international situation. In 1534 Charles acquiesced in the loss of Wurttemberg to the Protestants because he was preparing to attack the Turks in the Mediterranean.

The Schmalkaldic League grew in power throughout the 1530s. It established contacts with France, England and Denmark, while carefully preserving an appearance of loyalty to the Emperor. Charles was more concerned about relations with France and the Turks and, as a result, his policy in Germany throughout the l530s consisted of periodic denunciations of heresy combined with toleration in practice, while a solution was left to the General Council he repeatedly pressed upon the Pope. This absence of direction meant that the Protestants were able to make steady gains. By 1545 all of north east and north west Germany was Protestant, as well as large parts of the south. In 1544 Frederick II of the Palatinate became a Protestant. With all the secular Electors favourable to Protestantism and the Elector Archbishop of Cologne leaning in the same direction, the possibility of a Protestant Empire could no longer be ignored. It was time for Charles to take positive action. Fortunately for him, events had been moving in his direction for some time.

The Schmalkaldic League began to break up after 1540. From 1541 Landgrave Philip of Hesse, its most dynamic leader, was at the mercy of Charles V after he made a bigamous marriage (with the support of Luther) to avoid the sin of adultery! Bigamy carried the death penalty and so Philip was forced to support the Emperor. This gave rise to hopes for peace at the Diet of Regensburg in 1541. Two months of amicable talks between theologians of both sides failed to secure a compromise that either would accept. This was a turning point for Charles; he had based his whole policy on the idea of peaceful compromise and its failure left him bitterly disillusioned. Charles did not understand how strong religious passions were, especially on the question of the Eucharist. Issues that might have been peacefully settled by compromise twenty years before were now too deeply entrenched; only military victory or toleration would solve the problem now. As the latter was unacceptable in the long term to Charles, it left force as the only option.

Accordingly, Charles began to look for allies among the princes, but in the meantime he remained outwardly conciliatory in order to secure the help of the Protestants for the last war against Francis I. In the Peace of Crépy (1544), Francis not only agreed to co-operate over the calling of a General Council but also not to form alliances with the German Protestants. Suddenly they were isolated and Charles increased his advantages by making important alliances. The support of Bavaria was secured by promising Ferdinand's eldest daughter for Duke Albert's eldest son. Most important of all, the Protestant Duke Maurice was promised the Electorate of Saxony if he went over to Charles. For once the Pope (Paul III) was in full support of the Emperor and was generous with troops and money. All was now prepared for full-scale war against the heretics. Already, in 1543, a campaign against the Duke of Cleves had forced him to abandon the reformation of his territories.

A Venetian ambassador at the court of Charles V reviewed the situation in

July 1546:

> Concerning the Emperor's disposition towards the States of Germany, everyone is at present certain that war is in contemplation. . . The causes which are said to have moved the Emperor to this, are: first, the little regard which the German States have for some years past shown to his orders, by not attending the Diet; and secondly, the fear that the heresy which infects some of them, should spread over them all, and finally pervert his dominions in the Low Countries, which are the chief sources of his greatness. The Princes of Germany have never liked Charles V; probably because he continually avails himself of their counsels, without treating them in the deferential and considerate manner, which Maximilian and all the former Emperors accustomed them to expect. They complain that he has wasted power in disputes with his fellow Christians, instead of turning it to account against the Turk, as was his duty; that he is now about to make war upon themselves, and that under the pretence of religious zeal, he intends to conduct a foreign army into Germany, to trample on their ancient liberties.

1. What distinction can be drawn between the motives for war attributed to Charles V and what the princes believed to be the case?
2. From jour reading on Charles V so far, do you think the princes' fears were justified?

13. Resort to Force

The Schmalkaldic League was slow to realise that Charles had changed his policy. This was partly because they had no wish to fight the Emperor. Luther's insistence on obedience to secular rulers was part of his appeal to the princes but also made it harder for them to challenge their own overlord. The Emperor's troops were being assembled from the middle of 1545, but it was not until September 1546 that his army from the Netherlands, Hungary, different parts of the Empire and Italy was united. The failure of the League to win a quick victory before the armies united demonstrates their lack of effective leadership. There was no common ultimate objective and considerable distrust existed between the cities (who refused to pay for the troops) and the princes.

Charles won control of south Germany with little difficulty. Then in April 1547 he took the Lutherans by surprise and at the Battle of Muhlberg he crushed the army of the League, captured Elector John Frederick and gave his electoral title and the land which went with it to Maurice of Saxony. Mühlberg gave Charles control of the whole of Germany and his triumph was completed when Philip of Hesse surrendered in June. Germany was at his mercy; Francis I, Henry VIII and Luther were all dead. It seemed as if Charles could do as he pleased.

Paradoxically, the very completeness of his triumph ensured that it would be temporary. The Pope had already withdrawn his support and Catholic princes were not prepared to see Charles consolidate his ion at the expense of the Protestants if it would also adversely affect own power. Charles had shown his strength in combination with a number of the princes but if they all combined against him, he was powerless to enforce his will. Charles' position had been untenable from start. An alliance with the Protestant Duke Maurice in a religious war was always bound to break down.

A Diet was summoned to Augsburg in the autumn of 1547 and the Emperor proposed the formation of a league of princes with himself at the head, in which each member would contribute to the cost of a standing army to enforce the laws of the Empire. This was not a new idea—it was based on the earlier Swabian League—but it was defeated for the opposition of the princes who recognised how much Charles would be strengthened. The Elector of Brandenburg summed up their feelings: the Empire 'would be reduced to servitude'.

The religious question was also unresolved. The General Council at Trent, which first met in 1545, was a disappointment for Charles because it was not seeking a compromise solution to the Protestant problem, but a restatement of the Catholic faith in opposition to Protestantism. Charles attempted to solve the German problem himself Lw drawing up the 'Interim', a compromise which allowed clerical marriage and communion in both kinds; but there were no substantial concessions and the Interim was disliked by everyone. The Pope saw it as an attack on his own position and rights, while for the Protestants it was a wholly inadequate address to the depth of their religious convictions.

This double failure by Charles to resolve the political and religious problems of the Empire made him consider the future in a new light. The victory at Muhlberg had only been possible with the help of money and troops from the Netherlands and Spain. Any future Emperor deprived of these resources would find governing the Empire even more impossible than Charles himself. Such reasoning led Charles to question the position of his brother Ferdinand and, in so doing, to split the Habsburg family down the middle.

14. Dynastic Quarrels

Ferdinand had been granted the hereditary Habsburg lands in Austria and the Empire in 1522 by the treaty of Brussels, although Charles retained nominal rights in them. At the same time Charles had promised to work for Ferdinand's election as King of the Romans which would give him the right to succeed Charles as Emperor; a promise that was fulfilled in 1531 after Charles' coronation as Emperor. Since then, Ferdinand had been Charles' devoted regent, putting his brother's interests above his own even when there was serious danger, especially from the Turks. This was not easy for a proud and ambitious man but Ferdinand recognised that his power had come from Charles and that he gained from the latter's prestige as Emperor. Relations between the brothers had been especially good during the l540s and in the Schmalkaldic War. It therefore came as a great blow to Ferdinand when Charles proposed that his own son, Philip, should succeed Ferdinand as Emperor instead of the latter's son, Maximilian. In this way Charles felt that the two sides of the dynasty could be kept closely linked and Spanish resources could be made available for Imperial purposes.

This provoked a bitter family quarrel. Eight months of negotiations at Augsburg, 1550—51, eventually produced the Augsburg agreement in which Ferdinand accepted the idea of alternating the succession in the Empire between the two branches. The agreement did not please Maximilian or the princes, who felt their rights as Electors were being ignored and who were not prepared in any case to accept the succession of Philip who was a foreigner with no knowledge of Germany. The level of opposition was such that eventually Philip renounced his right to succeed Ferdinand. In return, Milan was detached from the Empire and added to the Spanish kingdoms. Charles had alienated his brother to no purpose and at a time when he was to face the most serious challenge to his power.

15. The Revolt of the Princes

Charles' cavalier attitude to the rights of the Electors and his humiliating imprisonment of John Frederick of Saxony and Philip of Hesse produced fears about the future liberties of the princes which sparked off revolt. The northern princes formed themselves into a league in 1550, for the defence of Lutheranism and the liberation of Philip of Hesse. This became much more dangerous for Charles when Maurice of Saxony joined, having not received the bishoprics of Halberstadt and Magdeburg which he had been promised. Also the Protestant princes secured the alliance of Henry II of France in return for the bishoprics of Metz, Toulon and Verdun. Such a combination had always been Charles' greatest fear but for a long time he refused to take seriously the reports of a movement against him. His contempt for the princes after Muhlberg convinced him that they would never dare to attack him.

Accordingly he left any preparations for war much too late. Maurice took the city of Magdeburg and Henry II walked into the Rhine bishoprics with no effective opposition. Charles was nearly captured in Innsbruck in May 1552 and the humiliation of flight gave him a shock from which he was unable to recover, although in the short term he showed great resolution in mustering resources from the one territory that could supply them—Spain. Charles now distrusted Ferdinand but had no-one else to rely on to negotiate with the princes. Peace within Germany became vital as the external threats mounted. The pirate Dragut was terrorising Naples, Ferdinand became involved in another Turkish war in Hungary, with French help the Imperial garrison was driven out of Siena and there were hostilities on the Flemish border.

Maurice of Saxony was also ready to negotiate because he lacked the resources to follow up his victory over the Emperor. In August 1552 temporary agreement was reached iii the Treaty of Passau. Charles was not prepared to accept the existence of Lutheranism as inevitable and permanent; the furthest he would go was to offer a truce in religious matters until the next Diet. Maurice and his allies were compelled to make do with this and attention could then be turned to the French.

The failure of the siege of Metz (November 1552—January 1553) was a bitter blow to Charles. He had hoped to drive the French out of the Empire and then resolve the problems in Germany by force. This was now impossible and the scale of his problems outstripped his resources. Even the long-suffering Castile could do no more—its revenues were already anticipated for the next three years. In the Empire the rule of law had broken down and Albert Alcibiades of Prussia, described as 'an enormous, insane, wild beast', was able to terrorise the country. Deeply disillusioned and with a feeling that God had deserted him, Charles decided that he was unable to solve the problems of the Empire and he must withdraw from it. In January 1553 he went to the Netherlands and never returned to Germany. The final acts of the reign were to be Ferdinand's although Charles' abdication was not accepted by the Electors until 1558.

16. The Peace of Augsburg

The first priority was to restore order. Leagues were formed which included both Catholic and Protestant princes. In July 1553 Albert Alcibiades was defeated at the battle of Sievershausen by Maurice of Saxony who was fatally wounded. Order was restored but only because the princes had wanted it. The reliance of the Emperor on the power of the princes was made plain, but so was their commitment to the continuing existence of the Empire and their willingness to preserve it. Ferdinand recognised that he could not coerce the princes within their own territories and this acceptance of political reality made the solution ilthe religious problem a possibility.

The Diet met at Augsburg in February 1555. Charles refused to attend: 'My reason is only this question of religion, in regard to which I have an unconquerable scruple'. In April 1555 he repeated his position to compromise, protesting against anything which 'could infringe, hurt, weaken or burden our ancient true Christian and Catholic faith'. In theory, this absolute stand was the position of both sides at the Diet. The ultimate aim was Christian unity but in the meantime, peace was a temporary necessity. The Catholics recognised they could not subdue the Lutherans by force, while the latter felt that their faith would become universal once it was freed from persecution.

The final solution was not tolerant in any real sense. It made provision only for Lutherans and Catholics, ignoring the growing strength of the Calvinists. Each prince was allowed to choose his own religion and thus determine the faith of his subjects—summed up in the formula cuius regio, eius religio (his territory, his religion). There was to be no missionary activity or protection of co-religionists in other territories. No territory ruled by a bishop which was Catholic in 1552 was allowed to become Protestant.

This pragmatic solution subordinated religion to politics. It was only possible in a nation such as Germany which had little real unity. Religious unity was preserved—but only within the bounds of each principality. More than anything else, this destroyed the medieval concept of the unity of the Empire and opened the way for the destructive conflicts of the next century.

Charles regarded his defeat in the Empire as his greatest failure and, on his own terms, it was.

17. The Abdication of Charles V

After his defeat at Metz, Charles sank into apathy and despair. He was aroused by the death of Edward VI in July 1553 and the succession of the still unmarried Mary. This gave rise to the possibility of leaving Philip with an empire that would revolve around Spain, England and the Netherlands, effectively strangling the hated France. This was a worthy inheritance for his beloved son and Charles felt he could then abdicate with a clear conscience. His plans had to be postponed for a time, however, because Henry II launched a savage attack upon Hainault in 1554. But then events in 1555 convinced Charles he must go. His mother died in April, Mary turned out to be barren, the religious peace of Augsburg was agreed in Germany and the new Pope, Paul IV, was fanatically anti-Spanish. To Charles, it seemed as if the same problems were reappearing and that he had failed in all his objectives.

On 25th October 1555, in the great hail of the castle at Brussels where he had begun his reign, Charles V abdicated with great solemnity: the crowd 'could not restrain their tears and sobs'. In a private ceremony in January 1556 he renounced his rights to Spain. He continued as Holy Roman Emperor in name only until February 1558 when the Electors agreed to choose Ferdinand instead.

Charles retired to Spain with his sisters Mary and Eleanor. He built himself a modest house near the remote monastery at Yuste and there he died in September 1558.

18. Charles V—A Failure?

Charles V was one of the great figures of his time. 'His personal moral character towered far above that of the princes of his age.' (H Holborn) He took the highly unusual step of abdicating voluntarily, feeling that his reign had been a failure, which in itself shows his integrity. Charles undoubtedly did fail in his two main objectives of suppressing heresy and leading a crusade against the Turks but this should not blind us to his achievements. The Turkish menace was withstood; Lutheranism had to be accepted as permanent but German Catholicism was saved at a crucial moment and revived in the latter part of the century; the Papacy saved partly by Charles' vision of Emperor and Pope leading a united Christendom together, despite the bad relations that often existed between them. 'His weakness did not diminish the geniuneness of that gesture which was of a piece with his lifelong attitude to his work. Charles' own attitude towards his office revived respect for the religious side of the imperial dignity.' (Francis Yates).

Charles' real failure as a ruler lay not in the inability to achieve his ideals, which were unrealisable, but in the legacy he left to his successors. He aimed for peace but the nature of his empire was such that the other powers in Europe could not tolerate it. Peace could only be obtained by unity or a balance of power. The resultant warfare, which was an almost constant backdrop to the reign, distorted the economies of Spain and the Netherlands and in the latter caused serious unrest. In Germany the Imperial title was preserved but only with the failure to gain real power and the effective fragmentation of the Empire.

Charles was a man of ideals with a deep sense of religious calling and purpose. He told Philip to 'exterminate heresy, lest it take root and overturn the state and social order' and he sought for peace so that he could purge the stain of heresy from his lands. Throughout his reign, the prize of victory seemed to come within his grasp (e.g. in 1525, 1530 and 1547) only to be snatched away by a new combination of forces working against him, fearful of his power.

The tragedy of Charles V was that he had a vision of Christendom united under one Pope and one Emperor working in harmony, which the extent of his dominions appeared to make a real possibility. In reality, the very power that he wielded was so threatening to others that it led to constant division and warfare, precisely what Charles sought to avoid. Vision and failure were inextricably interwoven from the start and it was no disgrace when Charles realised this and abandoned the struggle to men whose responsibilities were less and whose vision was narrower.

19. Bibliography

A F Alvarez *Charles V: Elected Emperor and Hereditary Ruler* (Thames & Hudson, 1975).

H G Koenisberger, *New Cambridge Modern History Vol. 2* (Chapter X) (CUP, 1959).

Karl Brandi *The Emperor Charles V* (Harvester, 1980).

J Lynch *Spain Under the Habsburgs Vol. 1* (2nd edition, Blackwell, 1981).

H Kamen *Spain 1469-1714: A Society of Conflict* (Longman, 1983).

H Holborn *A History of Modern Germany: The Reformation* (Knopf, 1959).

20. Discussion Points and Exercises

A. This section consists of questions or points that might be used for discussion (or written answers) as a way of expanding on the chapter and testing understanding of it:

1. Why is 'monarchia' a more accurate name for Charles' territories than 'empire'?

2. What mistakes by the young King prompted the revolt of the Comuneros?

3. What were the results of the Comunero revolt for a) the Cortes, b) the nobility?

4. Draw up a balance sheet of the gains and losses for Spain resulting from Charles' rule.

5. Could Charles be held responsible for the long series of wars against France?

6. Why was the Genoese alliance so important to Spain?

7. Why were the Turks such a problem for Charles V?

8. 'More of a burden than a privilege.' Is this a reasonable view of the Imperial title?

9. Why did Charles wait so long before taking decisive action against the Protestants?

10. Explain why the victory at Muhlberg led to the revolt of the Princes.

B. Essay questions

1. Why did Charles V encounter opposition within the Holy Roman Empire? How successful was he at overcoming this opposition?
2. To what extent were Charles V's problems of his own making?
3. 'A resounding success.' Is this a fair judgement of Charles V's rule as King of Spain?
4. Why did Charles V never create a unified administration for his empire?
5. Was Charles' conception of his role as Emperor unrealistic in the sixteenth century?
6. What were Charles V's aims against the Turks and how far did he realise them? (See Chapter X to help with this answer.)

21. Essay Writing—Discussion Essays

Many A-level essays have the word 'discuss' before or after a statement or quotation. Variants include 'comment' or 'do you agree?' but they are all the same type of question and are inviting a 'yes/no' answer. If a one-word answer makes sense, it is a discussion essay, e.g.: "A resounding success". Is this a fair judgement of Charles V's rule as King of Spain?' Note that in this example 'discuss' or 'comment' is not included in the title. You may have strong views on the question asked but the examiners would not have asked the question unless there was an opposing case, so even though you should express at least qualified support for one side or the other, it is essential to look at both sides. To put it another way, you must do the 'yes' and the 'no' side.

For this type of question, examiners often choose areas of current controversy among historians. If you have familiarised yourself with recent interpretations on a topic and can demonstrate your knowledge of leading ideas, this will be a great advantage.

Planning a 'yes/no' essay is relatively easy as a structure is already provided since you must consider each side in turn. If the question is in two parts, each of these must also have a 'yes' and 'no' side. In your conclusion you should then explain which side of the argument you favour and why.

Consider this question: "More a Mediterranean Monarch than a European Emperor" Discuss this view of Charles V.'

(a) To plan the essay, first assemble arguments with supporting evidence in favour of the statement.

(b) Next, assemble arguments with supporting evidence against the statement.

(c) Having assembled your arguments, you must arrange them in order. There are two ways of approaching this. Either put the 'yes' case first with arguments ranked in order of importance and then do the same for the 'no' case; or weave the two together—this can be more difficult as there are seldom times when there is a straight alternative but if you can link the contrasting views throughout the essay, it will make more effective reading.

Finally you come to the writing of the essay. Use your introduction to explore the difference between a Mediterranean Monarch and a World Emperor, i.e. what it is the examiner wants you to contrast. Then follows the bulk of the essay with the argument for each paragraph clearly stated in the first sentence and followed by some selected supporting evidence (you are not giving Charles' life history). From your weighting of the essay, one should be able to tell which side you are favouring. In your conclusion you must then state what your answer to the question is, with any reservations.

THE END

Published by Horsham House
www.horshamhouse.com

Rhythm and Swing by Sir Richard Hadlee
The Life of Abraham Lincoln
Great Expectations by Charles Darwin
Renaissance Europe by John Lotherington
Hittel on Gold Mines and Mining
The Odyssey of Homer
Stars of the Opera by Mabel Wagnells
The Hymns and Hymnwriters of Denmark
The War of the Worlds by H. G. Wells
Scottish Ghost Stories by Elliott O'Donnell
The Golden Threshold by Sarojini Naidu

Plus thousands more fiction and non-fiction titles

17359471R00022

Printed in Great Britain
by Amazon